CW00382908

FAKE FRIENDS

VS

REAL FRIENDS

HOW TO RECOGNIZE THEM

BY

Human Illustrations

© **Copyright 2020 by Human Illustrations**
All rights reserved.

This document is geared towards providing exact and reliable information with regards to the topic and issue covered. The publication is sold with the idea that the publisher is not required to render accounting, officially permitted, or otherwise, qualified services. If advice is necessary, legal or professional, a practiced individual in the profession should be ordered.

- From a Declaration of Principles which was accepted and approved equally by a Committee of the American Bar Association and a Committee of Publishers and Associations.

In no way is it legal to reproduce, duplicate, or transmit any part of this document in either electronic means or in printed format. Recording of this publication is strictly prohibited and any storage of this document is not allowed unless with written permission from the publisher. All rights reserved.

The information provided herein is stated to be truthful and consistent, in that any liability, in terms of inattention or otherwise, by any usage or abuse of any policies, processes, or directions contained within is the solitary and utter responsibility of the recipient reader. Under no circumstances will any legal responsibility or blame be held against the publisher for any reparation, damages, or monetary loss due to the information herein, either directly or indirectly.

Respective authors own all copyrights not held by the publisher.

The information herein is offered for informational purposes solely, and is universal as so. The presentation of the information is without contract or any type of guarantee assurance. The trademarks that are used are without any consent, and the publication of the trademark is without permission or backing by the trademark owner. All trademarks and brands within this book are for clarifying purposes only and are the owned by the owners themselves, not affiliated with this document

Table of Content

INTRODUCTION

It is very important to have friends in today's society. If not, the planet might be an ancient, large solitary place. But, how many of our mates are real or false. We also made fake friends, no matter whether or not you know that. Perhaps you were a fake friend yourself once. We can't sit now and turn and doubt our heads. Fake friends arrive, it's true, but they have to go. The distinction between a real and a fake friend at first can be difficult to understand. But, as soon as you know the difference, try to make and keep friends.

It might be tough for you to make friends because you are shy or inherently silent. It may be difficult to speak with people you do not know, or who makes you feel uncomfortable, even if you aren't shy. Sure, many teens feel nervous sometimes and some people feel timid other times. When you don't like to chat, there is nothing wrong with keeping to yourself.

You must be nice if you want mates. Which means that you are compassionate, patient and able to speak and understand.

It isn't really a dialogue to speak without listening. It's only the heart and mouth exercise. You definitely aren't going to make or hold many friends because you don't listen to the person you're talking to.

Another way to have mates is through sharing. Once you start talking, just keep them talking about yourself to others. When you say more about yourself, other children are more inclined to talk for themselves. Sharing also involves asking someone what your views, interests, intentions and emotions are.

Finally, you will speak politely to others and to others and be courteous in order to be friendly. Thank you and forgive me, it's very important to say things like sorry. It also means respecting and treating people as you would like. No one wants to be bossed.

1

Sometimes you have to be self-confident, and sometimes you even need to speak in a strong voice to people to prevent them from doing harm. But you could be respectful even then. Good, friendly communication is one way of generating happiness.

Kind voice is also more than that. Kind talk is about empowering others with your words. It means offering words of support and heartfelt praise to others for people who are lonely or sad. You will convince friends that by your words you really care for them. Kind speech, particularly when you do not expect it, brings dignity to someone's life through your words. But it could be even more. These will even bring empathy when doing positive deeds for others.

Many people in your life try to reduce your abilities. There's someone you know. Such criminals must be detected and stopped like the pestilence. Their existence alone will have catastrophic effects on you as they try to subvert you from your true life goals. You do your best to forget and go out if you have bad friends. If you're fictional, being alone is much easier than being a jokesman. You don't need mates.

Real friends come into our lives to show us things, to give us business. No matter what you both go through, a real friend will stick around; they will also help you go through these things together. A true friend is always there to help you grow and become a better person and a real friend.

You learn how to make and keep friends by taking these steps. But you're also going to learn who can and cannot trust your friendship. Both are necessary to be self-confident and assertive.

CHAPTER ONE

How to Identify a Fake Friend

Most people have problems identifying if any people's intentions are genuine or not, which leads to them discovering that many fake people travel and their self-interest is promoted. Friendship is not easy to build and requires a great deal of respect and love to accept and love others for all of them. What is the point if things are not like that? The keys to find and get a phony pal out of his life are here, so it's easier to be single than in bad company.

1. It takes a long time to create a strong bond when someone tries to be the closest friend overnight. Like with intimacy, trust and reverence are slowly acquired and not given.

Fake people tend to act as if the minute you encounter them, they were mates, so be aware!

2. Some of the best ways to identify a fake friend is to note them emerging in your life: if you are okay, happy, having a good time, they're going to make you join in their happiness and fun, so if the situation isn't so motivating you're going to lose that friend. In good times only empty people want to be there.

3. A false friend is someone who has an unintended opinion about your life (individual or professional). They will not miss the opportunity to point out your mistakes, to remind they that you lost and that you feel bad; because they will revel in your shortcomings anyway.

Fake people think about themselves, so they can either compliment you or make you look like trash before others.

4. A true buddy asks you in your profile and not behind your back what they think of you. We can promise that this person isn't a good company if you are sure this person lives objectively against others but never had the courage to tell you these issues in front of you.

5. Friendship means loyalty, and if a person constantly makes you feel wrong, does not value your views or decisions and is not a good friend or even a good party business, then interaction with them is better limited.

6. Fake people are envious who want to get what you have to learn from your popularity or people that are invasive and do nothing but place their nose in your company without telling them. They don't want to leave those negativity spaces, who continuously have a negative face in what you do.

7. You definitely have to face a fake friend if your partner makes you feel bad because you don't get hanging out any more, or if you plan to abandon all else because he or she wants something in particular.

8. We always suspect that someone isn't a good person and thus a poor friend, but that we have little courage to break this friendship. Beware of your instincts.

If you think somebody doesn't work for you, and if there is any difference between you then don't get close to that guy. Fake people sometimes come to ask for help, so be tired if you find that they are not coming to you for odd reasons.

Qualities That Make A Good Friend

When it comes to partnerships, certain people may be closer to you than others, which is good. Whereas some acquaintances might be in the area of "casual information," others might be in your inner circle. Obviously, there are many characteristics of good friends, and perhaps many of them are your nearest ones. There are many different ways, but one big way is that you're confident with the other guy, "says researchers, who are you without any fear of judgment. Furthermore, if this relationship actually helps all of yourselves as the most meaningful friendships make, then your closest friends are willing to be just who they are with you." Below, experts decide on the traits that make you –and your mates–a good friend, so you can see how they compare.

1. They're credible.

As a cornerstone and as a central quality, any partnership must have trust, and that is valid even for good friends. "They are sincere and trustworthy. "They are presenting us with a sounding board, testing our thoughts and revealing ourselves while not betraying our confidence or accusing us of our vulnerability." "They supply us with soulful and truthful encouragement, even if it hurts." It increases our self-esteem and helps you and the world to create a safe environment. "A good friend is someone you can trust, and don't share the personal information you share with anyone, or you can whisper about it, and trust your kids as well as your mate as a sibling; sometimes more than a member of the family."

2. They are compassionate. We are supportive.

It is necessary to have a support system and supporting friends are crucial. "Good friends give us different kinds of services, including helping physically, while we feel unsecure and supporting information in order to be able to deal with problems or ambiguities."It gives us energy and motivation to meet the many challenges of life and help us, if possible."

3. As you are, they welcome you.

Perhaps your good friends are confident because you can be with them; you can bring more of a front with others or be less easy.

"A good friend is someone who will welcome you unconditionally, but will never be afraid to tell you the negative reality of a situation or your actions,' They're a mirror which keeps your life centered when you lose perspective.' Researchers say that a great friend is someone with whom you believe you can share it and don't worry about exposing your vulnerability or disappointment. Some friends and rivals might do this, but it is a good friend who has the best chance of doing it in such a manner that they absorb and internalize

5

it properly. "You shouldn't judge them until your partner commits an awful crime," she says. "None of us is left untouched by something we would like to forget about this planet."

4. You are listening correctly.

A mate, though listening to what you have to say, consciously listens to a good friend. "A true friend is someone you cannot count on, but who asks questions and listens the answers truly," "They're not a coach, they're a listening board and they won't give you advice, because anyone is asking for you to listen."

5. We are available emotionally.

With an emotionally willing intimate partner, there are always good friends, hopefully. It helps one to share your own experiences with them and be connected, both combating isolation and helping to deal with distressing conditions. "It is what makes us feel understood and respected and our views: "We feel listened to and enjoyed, rather than overlooked and dismissed."

Naturally, some of your best friends don't live in the area, but you still have close contact. "There must be no good friend who is physically close to emotional involvement,' Physical closeness is a lot, but there are ways to stay together, especially today, even when you are really distant.' Those priorities are similar.

6. They Have Similar Interests.

Odds are, because you have some things in common you and your good friend(s). "The principles, beliefs and opinions are close to us on subjects which matter to us," says the researchers. Researchers. "We feel a sense of identity that fulfills the fundamental human need to feel connected to others. We are united, together and feel a sense of being a part of it"

7. During the hard times, they show up.

Although it's convenient for someone to be there during the good times, being there for them during the good ones is even more awesome. "Good friends are showing up in hard times," says the report. We help you clean up after the party, come to the funeral of your parent and escort you from the appointment of that psychiatrist you've been scared of. All good memories are easy to build, but the true test of a relationship is these crucial times."

8. They're mutual.

A good balance of gift and acceptance is important in every form of relationship. "Good friendships have reciprocity, so that you have a healthy, symbiotic relationship," says study "Sometimes you hold a ball and a friend sometimes does. This partnership is over when one hand is giving everything, "There are those in this world who take care of it and the donors," says Study. "Sometimes a friend gives much more than the other, and that is all right as long as the other person often reciprocates. Which perfect is this person for a friend if you are giving and they are only taking?"

9. You are the best they can think of.

At times, you can feel like you know better than you do yourself because your good friends meet you. "You speak in your own interest, but it won't benefit you. Good friends can be your biggest cheerleaders and champions, "They will represent you as responsible allies, keeping you centered even at moments when you doubt yourself and your self-worth." Good friends can constantly build you up, remind you of how amazing you are, and assist you in learning and growing in your life.

10. When you need anything you don't just reach out.

You can think about people who only contact you if they need something. But in fact, researchers say, good friends are in touch with you. "They follow you out to smile at you, 'only because they always have time to be there while you need them, not only for their spare time in a sacrificial way.'

11. They're loyal, they're getting you out, No matter what.

You know the buddy who dumps it all to assist you? This is a good friend's description. "They are there for us when we need them and improve our lives, lighten our burden and help us deal with the constant challenges and pressures of life. Friends will turn a small hill that is slowly climbing into what looks like an insurmountable mountain." A true friend is someone who supports you for much in exchange," he said.

In the same way, scientists often think they can tell who a good friend is, particularly in challenging times, on how trustworthy they are. "When you have a good friend and not so easy time, you will be standing by you," Reasecher says, "When you go through a traumatic experience like a divorce, they will stand by you, but many people lose support at this moment of difficulties.""A friend is a good friend and separates them from the others, as you can see. And if you think that you might be a better friend, it's good news, it's not too late.

Major Differences between Real Friends and Fake Friends

We are all looking for a lot of true friends, because friendship is really one of the best aspects of your life, but you ought to know that there are a lot of differences between real friends and fake friends. A fake and real friend can be quite difficult to distinguish, because there are different levels of intimacy, some not on the table.

Here are the main differences you need to remember between real friends and fake friends:

➢ **Support**

One of the major differences between real friends and fake friends is that you're helped by a true friend irrespective. You will be motivated by anything you do, even if they are not in compliance with your options and are always there thick and thin on your side.

➢ **Love you.**

A real friend would love you with all your flaws and virtues and embrace you exactly like you are. You know that you are not flawless; you know you may make some mistakes, but you are there, regardless. You know. We have dorky stuff that we frequently do. Instead of making fun of you, a real friend can join you.

A true friend always has the back, even though you're frustrated about something.

➤ **A true friend always has your back.**

If you're mistaken or what the problem is, it doesn't matter who's on the other side and you won't fight for you, no matter what. And, while they care about your insecurities, they will not move them on to others. they'll give you a shoulder when you need it.

➤ **They keep in contact.**

You just have to watch who holds you in constant contact when you want to figure out who your true friends are. Fake friends generally only ask you because they like or need anything from you and not if they necessarily want to know how you do it or if they want to go out. You don't really know what's going on in your life, and you often feel like they just call you because there was nobody else.

➤ **Keep your secrets.**

Your secrets will always be protected by a true friend, even though some of the things you have done might not be appropriate. You can trust them completely, because you know you can always depend on them. A true friend will respect your faith and will do all they can to make you happy.

➤ **Don't want to gossip.**

A good friend's most valuable attribute is that you don't want gossip. You can trust them fully and they won't talk behind your back or spread rumors that aren't real.

A false mate, on the other hand, talks in public about your unsafety, and even embarrasses you. Usually when you're around you, it's hard to be yourself.

➤ **A genuine friend always gives you time, whether busy or tired.**

A good friend always makes you time. They would even invite you to come over for a drink any time, even though they're home for just an hour. They enjoy spending time with you. You can sometimes even sit quietly and safely still. Actual friends know all the things that make you feel happy, they encourage you and they also advise you to pursue your interests.

Signs Someone Is Using You and What to Do About It

It hurts to know that someone you felt was close to uses you and really don't want to be a real friend. It is quick first to run away from the truth in cases like these, disregard the signs and exist in a denial state. The truth is, nothing will change until you confront the situation and take a good look at the actions of your friend.

Did you get a sinking feeling that sometimes your mate isn't so fond of you?

Do not feel too bad about this. Some people really are not able to really have a relationship and besides using men they don't know how to do anything else.

When you find one of your mates suits in with this definition, look at the following signs along with the strategies for dealing with the wrongdoer.

1. Your mate doesn't call you, unless they need something.

When your buddy needs you, the clearest indication is that they don't get in contact with you because they need something specific. At first, it might not be clear what they need because their purpose can be fairly self-aware.

For examples, your friend might be calling you to hang out. You spend a lot of hours with you and occasionally they chat about a problem. Maybe their vehicle collapsed, maybe they needed to cut an overgrown tree in their front yard or the washing money was short.

You're not going to be asked for anything by an experienced customer. They will draw up a report and then address the problem. You may give them a ride to work until you become aware of this, to fallen with their chainsaw their tree, or to let them use your washer and dryer.

Obviously, doing good for your mates is nothing bad—this is part of friendship! The problem begins when almost every time you see your friend wants something from you.

2. They Do Everything They Can to Give You as Little as Possible.

The whole idea, when someone exploits you, is that they get away with the "friendship" more than you. We go against their agenda if it's too much or worse, whether we offer more than you do. For them to "use" your friendship, you probably have to do more over the long term.

First of all, consider if they are ready to offer you the same kind of favor. Many strong partnerships are supported by people, although they are often negative. But are you the only one who leaves you?

Only want to see how you commit to anything of the same basis that they appear to ask.

Do not inquire for something outrageous. Whether you repeatedly refuse to help or even feel ashamed to inquire, it's a bad sign.

Worse still, they may sometimes rashly satisfy your wishes, but they will not want to fix the dilemma, as they only try to appease you for reasons of aesthetics.

For instance, your bicycle may have snapshot and you need a way to function now. Installed in your garage for half a century, instead of simply trying to fix the problem by sending you a lift or a bus ticket, your mate is selling a rusty old wheel, with flat tires.

They might say, "I have helped you," but they don't need to spend much time or resources to take care of their lives and problems. In truth, this leads to the next symbol.

3. They don't ever worry of you.

We never seem to care about you unless you need something. They don't tend to call you at holidays; they don't tend to bring you presents when they go on a vacation and, as a result, they don' t hear this one album that I think you'll enjoy!

You have little consideration, and they hardly ever think about you... until they worry about how to get out of you. There are almost always thoughtless mates who use there.

4. Your friend knows little about you, shockingly.

Another indication that someone trusts you is clearly because you just don't care. After all, you don't know first of all about it.

If your "mate" seems to be not paying great attention to your messages, forgets important things about you, and seems uninterested in general, so they clearly have to stick with you for another cause. It's more than just forgetful.

5. They speak of you badly to others.

Any people cannot just stop gossiping. It's real. This is like alcohol. It is like addiction. However, one of the attributes of a customer is that they will not worry of tossing you under the bus twice. If you're not there, because they really know not about your credibility, they'll talk badly to you.

Nonetheless, they're not mates with you for their lovely personality if they have lots of grievances about you and hang on you.

6. They are gone when you have a crisis.

Have your lives been abruptly swept away by something you need? Often it's not even about money or resources— often; when our world falls apart, we might just need someone to talk to.

Will your mate stand up with you when something horrible happens? Or just crickets chirping, you hear?

Another thing is that if you're a Negative Ned and lament in your life about everything you do–it pushes others away. But you should be able to wait for a real friend if you are a reasonably good person in an emergency.

7. In specific circumstances, you hang out only.

Sometimes the situations will obscure the fact that your friend needs you. For e.g, if you go to your favorite nightclub, you may only meet each other. If you are famous and making them feel nice to be seen with you, then it may be difficult to tell if they are using you to gain their social status!

Turn a little stuff up. See if your friend is willing to hang out or do something entirely different. If your buddy doesn't like this game, he should be happy to spend time with you, when he needs you.

8. If you don't give them what they want, they are pushy or aggressive.

Good friends know the limitations. If you don't give in to your investigations, lousy buddies who only plan to use you for money can be furious. Some times, they can even try to manipulate you with remorse or say things such as, "I think you were my mate." Check this conduct regulation. Real friends should value your free will, even though you have nothing to offer aside from your friendship.

9. You've been told that you are being used.

That may sound too obvious, but it's sometimes not. A buddy who uses you many times will use his own guilt as an excuse.

I'm sorry, I guess that's what you mean. If somebody asks you that but makes no effort to change the way this they treat your relationship, they actually have convinced you themselves that they're using you. I know that I can't do anything, but they say that they're not going to be able to do anything. Listen to them, listen to them, listen to them!

10. They Always Need to Be in Charge.

The partner does not want to put your own point of view aside for a moment in order to see yours is a normal behavior pattern in someone who wants to cross you twice.

These people usually have to stay on their position although a rational approach is provided to justify why things should be done differently. You will often be humiliated because you don't live up to the wishes of your mate.

11. They Know All of Your Buttons and Push Them Accordingly.

Deceptive friends begin as someone who was interested in meeting you and is interested in your overall well-being. This will be until you have the opportunity to get over. Don't be shocked if you use your vulnerability or other sensitive information against you when this happens. Emotional manipulators know your feelings well and will use them against you rapidly.

CHAPTER TWO

Ways to Avoid Fake People

Man is an animal in culture. This is human nature when people are encircled by friends with whom you will exchange memories and experiences. But not all of the people you meet are real, always false people around you, who always act differently and want to stay away from you is the best thing to do.

Life is much better if malicious and false people from the world can be stopped. The more optimistic, honest people you have in your life, the higher the chances of meeting your goals are.

1. Limit your fake human contact.

There are circumstances in which people like this can't leave to meet them, but keep the conversations brief and avoid getting irritated or offended by their actions.

The less you feel discomfortable when you expend little or no time with the fake person. False people are mainly eager to pay attention and this guy you do not want to send. To make them feel confident for themselves, you do not involve them. That simply just exacerbates it. Validation means that they can continue to do so.

2. Don't let you receive their annoying conduct.

Regardless of how irritating and disturbing the actions of the individual may be, try to preserve your calm.

Do not let your acts get you the worst, no matter how mischievous it is. It's best to stop the conversation quickly and encourage yourself to cool down when you're in a situation that makes you worse. But when the fake person does something arrogant and insulting, it's not something that should be accepted. When it comes to false people's behaviour, don't be afraid to challenge them about their actions.

3. Do not stoop down to their level.

In other people you can't fight fakeness, either. Resist the tentation to "return" a fake person with gossiping and insulting remarks. But always in mind that you become the person you've said you dislike or stop if you act in this way.

4. Should not reveal your personal problems and secrets.

You would best refrain from exposing your deepest secrets to him / her if you believe that one of your mates behaves wrongly. You should do so gradually in order to prevent the person from getting a warning that you did not believe him. This helps you slowly to step away from the person and evaluate your relationship.

5. Take care of your own business.

Do not bother getting into the scenario if this guy does not communicate with you and all you have heard of being false comes from secondary knowledge. Concentrate about yourself for what you are doing. Until it affects you, then let it be.

6. Meet new people.-Meet new people.

The planet is too growing for fake people to threaten you. New friendships and relationships may seem frightening, but they are so much safer than being around men, who only have chaos and misery in their lives.

Stay optimistic and soon you will forget about these falsified people and you can grow many new friends in confidence and admiration. This is a certain way to avoid fake people in your main concern.

7. Face them.

Do not hesitate to challenge and point out these acts as you can't carry the things that the fake person is doing and impacts you at a whole other level. These criminals will continue to brush your life away if they are accepted all the time. We look for so much affirmation and can even make them realize their acts by calling out their wrongdoing.

8. Not everyone you lose is a loss.

Don't feel guilty or horrible about it because you lost a very good friend with their fakes. It's better to lose contact with someone who only brings negativity and misery in your life than being friends.

Self-love should be given greater importance because it fully affects your life.

9. Give them assistance. Offer them assistance.

When the false person is a close friend of yours and you find like you should communicate with them, please ask them what is happening and why are they doing this and seek to make them work on any of the issues they have raised. But don't be upset if they don't know or refuse to help. It is still their decision and what is important is that they have made an effort to understand their decisions and have helped them to cope with them. It is best to keep going and let them do what they want if this situation happens.

10. Keep in mind it's not about you yet.

Fake people's actions have nothing to do with you–they have everything to do with them. Notice always that you try to prove something to others and especially yourself, but most definitely you go away when you don't get the evidence that you need of other people. Do not participate as much as possible in relationships and always note that they lie to themselves and not to you or others. And while communicating with and engaging with such people is difficult, keep in mind that they are the ones who really are hurting.

It is very easy to be tempted to become something that we are not in our society today, where perfection or beautiful are represented, particularly in social media sites. Nonetheless, we should not adhere to our society's standards and just recognize who we are. As my

17

counsellor taught me, "Trusting yourself is easier than being loved." If you meet people of this kind, consider those tips so you can stop the poisonous and harmful energy that comes into your lives.

Things Fake Friends Do That Real Friends Don't

Even when the analog days were quite confined to friends, we realized that IRL was, not anybody's count of friends exceeded thousands. But, now when the word "people" has been the most momentary, casual contact we have ever had with Snapchat, Instagram, Diskord, or Twitter–well, we're all the more famous.

Then how does it not sound like that exactly? Nonetheless, in a 2019 survey conducted by analysts, 27 percent of millennials felt like they have no close friends, and most of the time three out of ten people feel lonely.

One thing is certain whether the social media allows us to interact or disconnect: a true friend is difficult to find. But how can you know who of your mates are real "keepers?" The researchers say that "true friends" ought to have their best interests at heart, stand up for you in your absence, keep up your lies, treat you with respect and be honest and supportive and be glad for your achievements?

➤ **Fake friends put you down.**

When your true friends see all of your amazing things and they love them, false enemies won't see them at all, or can feel insecure and try to pick you up. A deliberate observation teaches us that these downs that take the form of not - so-sweet mockery from backhanded compliments: "The jeans don't make you look anything like the cargo pants you were wearing last day," or of the infamous humble brag: "You're so lucky you can stay home on New Year's Eve.

 In the latter case, a true friend welcomes you or sits and shares a drink of champagne with you

➢ **False friends are there only if they like.**

Apparently randomly, fake friends tend to drop into and out of your life, but if you look at the history, it's not really as random as all that. Are you sick with influenza in bed or maybe feel a bit sad and hungry? Nothing in sight of a fake friend.

Will you get a bonus and a bigger payroll? Assume who's going to help you celebrate? This is the kind of friend who will most likely not care to answer your call or messages for a few days or weeks or even months if you are trying to contact us. (As long as you buy, that is.) Nonetheless, if this "mate" approaches you, you may be quite confident that you will be hit for a contribution or that you are being asked for some kind of favor.

➢ **Fake friends just want to talk about themselves.**

If you have a friend whose biography you can recite with your hands, but you are quite confident that it'd be difficult to call your favourite or even to ask how to coffee... Yup, warning fake buddy. You continue to be seen as a crowd by fake friends, because everybody knows that, after all, they are the only ones whose lives are of concern.

So should you ever have an issue, your empathically-impaired "mate" will see this only in reference to how they will benefit from it: "That's what you are thinking, the death of your mum is about to keep you from helping me move into my new apartments?"

➢ **Fake friends are saying that this is their way or the highway.**

Just one view, Fake Friends want to hear: its own. We don't condemn it, because it's all yes and women that they want, or a reflection that represents what they already want to be real. Wait for your "mate" to fight endlessly and try and win you over to a "right" side and, if you're not persuaded, you might no longer consider yourself a friend.

You might also believe you have had a lucky escape because, as Researchers put it, a relationship in which your views are disregarded is "evil with respect to your emotional and mental health." Is any one of these a bell?

A bell of warning, maybe? You may need to try to reduce the amount of time or at least the level of engagement you expend with a fake friend if you believe that you are dealing with him.

You can reduce your standards only if you intend to accept your goodness, much less reciprocation. You're just frustrated and disappointed. However, try not to feel too bad. It's just not you, it's them, mind. Personally, it would be better if you could just end the relationship. Allow yourself to be a lousy friend of someone else while you are making the true friends.

How To Stay Away From Fake Friends Them Before They Take Advantage Of You

False friends always take more than they can offer when it comes to relationships. Such a relationship won't give you any benefits, but will use you in any situation. You will rob your energy and feel exhausted. The signs that prove you have a false friend are here:

1. Is an opportunist.

Have you ever got a friend who's making plans with you a day later? Look out— this man might not be a true friend. She typically compiles three different things on one night; she chooses the best and at the last minute, she cancels the two other things. A good friend prioritizes your time with you (even if it is just a home movie night together that your plans include).

2. Only think about themselves.

The narcissists become fake friends more often than not. We have difficulty forming real ties, and we rely very much on ourselves. Healthy relationships involve giving and taking, but a phony partner takes your time and gives nothing in exchange.

3. Leverage for emotional support regularly.

Those emotionally insecure don't make the best friends everywhere. Although helping your friends is extremely important— particularly if they struggle with something — false friends would benefit from your willingness to learn. We are going to take you into an energetic sprint with no concerns about your specifications.

4. Gossips about others.

Here is a time. Here is a moment. When talking, certain people themselves concoct gossips just for a certain person to say something evil. Gossiping is not acceptable in any way, or someone who leads the conversation speaks badly about someone says a lot.

5. Mocks and thank you simultaneously.

They're going to cover a joke with a grin so they can annoy you and hold you close together. And they keep you going, but they still don't care about you. They are very effective negotiators and this manipulative tactic helps you to be exploited.

6. Makes you choose them over your friends.

Because you are so self-centered and independent, you would always try to make your servant available. You might have to have real friends, so don't get in the hole.

Warning Signs That Fake Friends Are Ruining Your Life

You are faithful and grateful to your friends? How many genuine friends are you? Maybe you know that just a few real friends are there. Many are wearing masks, but before they make you unhappy, you will notice toxic people. Here are the warning signs that ruin your life for your fake friends.

1. Lower your self-esteem Fake Friends.

21

You're nice and light-minded when you're young. It is more critical than consistency the number of your friends. You want to be encircled by people who like to go out. You become more aware with false friends as you grow up.

You're not your real friends, men who mock and threaten you. It's your poor appreciation. Sometimes they condemn you and only consider the faults.

Why does this happen? You feel bad for yourself, so try to make yourself look better if you are insulted. You should stop them rather than be upset at them. Their poor self-confidence isn't your fault. Even as they are far inside, they can't accept themselves. Nor do they embrace you surprisingly. All too often, once you better yourself, you get jealous.

Finally, if you need these fake friends in your life, you can ask yourself. Did you know how irritating they are? Your life is ruined. Surround yourself with great people who will add to your improvement.

2. They Hold You Back From Achieving Your Goals.

True friends are going to tell you how to accomplish your objectives. A success, too, will be. If you have issues, you will be helped and you won't be frustrated. They're not going to tell you why you can't achieve your goals. False friends, however, do not help you accomplish your objectives. If you think about your ambitions, you won't listen to you. Your success will not be honored.

You will soon stop discussing with them your milestones.

We are competitive? They are competitive? Take a look at what the goals are. Even your false buddies try to outdo you from work to marriages and other facets of your life. You will discourage people who keep you from attaining your targets if you want to succeed. You will consider a new business if you want to be happier.

3. Fake Friends Gossip About You.

You assume that everybody is as nice as you are as a young person. Don't expect people to expect too much. Some people just pretend to love you. You should recognize people that do not love you and that do not respect you. No reason to disrespect is open. When you're not present, you'll think negative stuff about you. Somebody may believe and stop their lies. Fake friends may threaten to ruin your romantic relationship or other friendship and make things worse. As quickly as possible, you should get rid of them.

4. They Make You Feel Guilty.

Did you feel like you drain the time from your friends? You know how to find the culprits? Far from everyone had to do with mates who were abusive. Such men claim to be involved in your best, all the while using deception to know what you want. You should play the victim, so that you seem to have created the dilemma you began. Friends of deception take your instincts, mental values and knowledge to heart.

You don't need them. You're only curious in what you can do. It is not really a relationship if you have a friend who takes you past events such as supporting you in a difficult time.

5. They Will Try to Ruin Your Relationships.

Have you a friend questioning your partner? Have you a friend who does not listen to you when you chat in a relationship about your romantic moments? If your life goes fine, your phony relationship goes downhill.

When you are any happier than they are, your false mates are jealous. You think they're worth more than you do. When you break up with your partner, you should rejoice. Fake friends will also try to ruin you. You'll let your life kill them?

You must know that life is not a fairy tale early or later. It doesn't guarantee they would regard you well if you treat other people well.

You're supposed to accept people, because you can't change anyone. It is tough enough to change yourself, so just imagine how difficult it is for somebody else to change. Love is acceptance. If you can't accept someone, particularly if it isn't true, you should stop hanging out with him. Save your friendship! Save your marriages!

Somebody who deserves your confidence is hard to find. You ought to be vigilant. When you stop fake boyfriends that destroy your life, your life will be much easier. Gladness and harmony are earned.

CHAPTER THREE

Signs Your Friend Is Trying To Break Up With You

They often see partnerships as life-long ties. But that's not always the case, unfortunately. You will begin to see the signs that your mate pulled away, or perhaps even "breaked" with you if your friendship is going, or something was between you and your beast.

Investigators claim that. "It could have been one or both of you who have outgrown your relationship. In many situations, marriages terminate because of serious new relationships or other life-length activities, like having children or getting a new career."

But that doesn't mean you should not seek to rekindle a fading relationship and re-establish yourselves. "I would suggest that you usually do what you can to preserve important partnerships that could die," says Researchers.

"You are able to do this by giving your friend more time and attention and contact. In many situations, though, your friend is going to simply move on. At this stage, the best way forward is to accept reality and try to meet the people who share your current values and who ideally will be faithful."

1. They don't see your future as fascinated.

It is not good indication if you and your mate used to write text 24 hours a day and share your life info with you vigorously when it comes to paying attention.

"If someone no longer wants to be your friend,[they] may not have the confidence to go specifically and tell you," researchers say. "That means fewer calls, a slow response or little attempt to pick up." Of course they could only be interested, or you might eventually fall into a new stage of your relationship, when you catch up on every day a couple times a year. The best way to learn what it might be is to ask and answer questions specifically about your concerns.

2. They Aren't Inviting You Out.

Don't worry if your friend often visits the city and doesn't invite them, they may forget to add your name to the group text, or they may think you wouldn't want to go. It's NBD most of the time. However, take note if you are more often than not omitted as this may be an indication your friend supports. "When you find that your partner is going out with new people, and you're never invited (via the social media or mouth) it's a sign that you're moving on from your relationship. To sort out what's up, you might want to invite their new friends and watch out for what happens.

Your partner is not always able to have that last' blow out fight' that ends up in marriage, "say researchers." Then there may be a lot of underlying resentment against you to trigger the desire to break up. If this is the case, it can save the partnership. What's crazy about them? What can you do to make matters smooth? If you ask, you can't solve the problem.

3. They're No Longer Opening Up To You.

If your friend is planning on hitting the old dusty trail, it makes sense why they might be less inclined to reveal their deepest, darkest secrets since these things are usually reserved for the tightest of pals.

That's why, "if you and your friend used to have honest, meaningful conversations about your lives and that lessens or stops, it could be a sign of trouble," Bennett says. "It probably means that your friend has found someone else to confide in or no longer values your friendship as highly." But hey, it's also possible they've run out of secrets to tells, so don't jump to conclusions.

4. They Keep Making Excuses When You Ask To Hang Out.

Sure, your friend may be going through a tough time, they may be tired, or they may simply be stressed out from work, so don't hold it against them if they need to bail on a hangout, or seem a little less available for a while.

It's only when you can't seem to ever nail them down, or they seem to be tossing ridiculous excuses your way, that you might want to raise an eyebrow. "If a friend is still taking your calls and answering texts, but is always coming up with excuses for why you can't get together," they may not want to make the effort anymore.

Of course, this isn't the best way to handle the situation, on their part. So you might want to speak up.

"If it starts to feel like the excuses are lame or not true, then you might want to tell the friend about your suspicions and ask if the friend's feelings about the relationship are changing," Researchers says. That way, you can get to the bottom of the issue, and save yourself from all that wondering.

5. They're Constantly Arguing & Complaining.

Has your best turned herself into someone who's impossible to be around? "If your friend does agree to get together with you, but the time together feels very negatively charged, full of complaining and picking fights with you, then they might be trying to get you to feel fed up and break up the relationship first.

Either that, "or there might be a lot of underlying anger towards you, motivating the desire to break up, and the friend doesn't feel ready to have that final 'blow out argument' that ends the friendship," Researchers says. When that's the case, calling them out may just save the relationship. What are they mad about? What can you do to smooth things over? You won't be able to fix the issue, unless you ask.

6. Whenever you hang out, they are quiet.

Alright, but everyone has the right to occasionally bad mood. But if you see a pattern that doesn't speak to your friend when you go for the brunch or if you visit her and she goes like you're not there, it could be a warning. It's like a phenomenon.

"As if your friend looks unhappy, you don't make contact with your eye and you don't feel anxious and tight in your body position, but you see this same friend smiling and looking happy when you are engaging with others, there is some stirring in your relationship," A genuine friendship shouldn't seem like a hostage situation.

7. They're Straight Up Avoiding You.

On the not-so-subtle side, if it seems like your friend is straight up avoiding you, that may be the final sign you need to confirm your suspicions. "If a friend is not answering your calls or texts and seems to 'never be around,' it could be that there is a lot going on in this friend's life, or it could be that they're trying to create distance in the relationship," Researchers says. "It may be that this friend wants to 'break up' with you, but doesn't know how to say it and doesn't want to have an awkward conversation or fight with you.

As in any relationship, endings can be emotional and difficult, so some people opt to ghost the other person, sending the message in a passive way."

The thing to keep in mind, if any of the above sounds familiar, is that friendships do come to an end. We often think of them as lifelong, but that isn't always the case. If you and your friend no longer see eye-to-eye, are entering different stages of life, or the friendship has simply run its course, it's more than OK to let that happen, and move onto new people, who will appreciate having you in their lives.

How To Deal With And Manage Friends Who Use You

Capitalism makes men commodities. Persons are limited to titles, net worth and are used merely as instruments for the benefit of the general and efficient economic process with all their complexities. It's difficult to know who your real friends are in this digital world and who they are. Most people are trained to put on a nice face, to say the right things and then leave when it gets tough.

More often than not, others want to communicate with you for selfish reasons if you are a successful person. They want to feel more fulfilled in your company. Your coworkers tend to network. They try to use you basically. I've discovered how impossible it is if money and power are intimately involved to make true friends.

And the fact is that when you slip, or who wants to leap over you, you don't always know who will extend a hand.

It's what makes it so hard— the bond between humans is a basic necessity. It is part of what makes life worth living and what makes it possible for your achievements to be shared with other people. It is therefore important to find out who you can trust, what viewpoints you can respect, and which people relate to you only for their own gain.

These are the simplest and most unexpected ways to say who your real friends are so you can optimize your commitment and let others go.

1. They help you celebrate your accomplishments.

They get jealous and nervous while you are surrounded by poisonous people. You will find no room in your hearts for your happiness, for your success strengthens your sense of failure. They cannot rejoice for you.

Encircle yourself with those who raise you. You want to glow real friends.

2. When you feel pain and difficulty, they notice and help you.

When times get tough, true friends don't abandon you. We've all got downs and ups. When you have a hard time–homelessness, divorce, death from your children, etc. – your real friends come to you. Tell yourself how you do. And offer to help you work through it to keep you from struggling alone.

3. They are asking you meaningful questions which most people don't think about.

That is significant. In your life, you can have many wonderful and encouraging people, but if they do not ask you meaningful questions, this friendship is hard to sustain and develop. Best friends help you make meaning and understand your heart-felt beliefs instead of just talking about things that are trivial and of no significance.

4. They listen deeply rather than waiting to talk about themselves.

It doesn't mean a good conversation when people constantly turn the focus back to themselves. It's a clever way to tell you that it doesn't matter so much that the background. True friends listen to you sincerely and speak to you. We send you the space you will feel respected and recognized.

5. They challenge you to grow (and they grow with you).

The best friends that you can have are those who inspire and motivate you to develop further as a human and a job in this country. You're shouting you out. You find out if you don't live up to your principles. And they want you to respect and appreciate the same level of love.

That kind of reciprocity helps you both to evolve together - irrespective of what else the friendship can affect. Surround yourself with people who fan the fires and do what they say.

An essential component of established, stable communication is every object mentioned above. As you read the list, somebody came to mind and you had to prioritize it, keep it at all costs. Don't allow your work's demands to separate you from the ideals and people that give meaning to your lives. Fight to keep your life full and enliven your spirit in friendships.

Ways To Bond With A Friend To Become Even Closer

Often you have a friend like other people you want to live with, even though you can't quite call him a "friend close." It's great. You both have fun to hang out whenever you see each other, and maybe you can do something without a lot, so you can't call them when you need a wind-up person or just turn up at their house and feel comfortable there instantly. And while not every partner must ever be your best friend, you may want to make that particular relationship the next step. If so, there are some ways of getting closer to a partner than you already are.

It can take time to switch from "friend" to "mate" or "best friend." You and the individual often simply click, and you get on the hip right away. On other days the partnership is a little slower, so that's all right too.

Bonding doesn't happen to everybody naturally: I know that first-hand as a shy girl who often finds it difficult to open up to people.

➢ **Express both bad and good stuff.**

Somebody to share something positive with is one of the great things about making friends.

Nonetheless, a good friend is one of the best things you can do with the bad things. That's how close friends and strangers vary from one another. You will learn to open up to them if you want to come closer to someone.

➢ **Towards Find out what you've got in common.**

31

It can almost feel like dates often moving closer and closer to a partner, you're not sure what to do with each other, it don't want to do or say the wrong thing or you don't know exactly what you do because the person's not really nice yet.

So as you try to link up with your mate and get closer, you're going to have easy hangouts about what you will and do. Researchers said, "When you like things outside, or come from the same part of the city, invite them to do something they would like to do, too."

It might seem easy clearly to say "listen to them," but it's something other people are grappling with even though they don't realize. Be extremely careful when your friend is chatting, and listen to them sincerely when we get to meet a person and listen to him. We do not participate in society today, but rather are trapped in the world of our own. A close friend will see you genuinely develop a relationship, truly listening. "In other words, when you are together put your phone down and pay full attention to them and don't really interrupt them with your own advice or story.

➤ **Keep things simple.**

Once, it may be close to arranging a hang-out with a new friend on a third or fourth day.

You don't have to undo stuff or try to do anything stupid when you get together. Keep it clear and don't try too hard!

You will feel anxious before you even hang out and just get on with it if you only talk about what you want. Start with small things—dinner or stroll to the market of farmers... don't search too fast for too much nice time. That's natural."

➤ **Always be yourself.**

Again: try not too hard. Now. Another person will take another up if you are not honest and it might be a change. It happens not only to talk, but also together to make plans. "That does not mess with your work or career, Roberts said. I know many women who have stayed silent to feel fit for new friends.

You can't afford to go to expensive meals, weekends away that are nervous because you are not too close yet, or hang out more late than the body wants you to make them believe that you are someone you aren't. When the right individual and one who loves you build a solid foundation, so they can truly appreciate that you cannot stop or intend to go home in the early future. When she doesn't, she's not someone for whom you really want, right?

➢ **Don't compare your new friend to older friends.**

You could equate this relationship to those if you had bad friends before–and no one can do so equally. Roberts wrote, "She's not your ex, even as she's in romantic relations. Do not dump on her your old cravings." Remember: it's a different person and she won't be the same as your last friend.

Another thing you can note is the amount of garbage that your old friends are dreaming about. "You'll probably link your ex-friends further, but make sure you don't harder to take them off. It sends the message you can do the same for her. Don't talk to her about the guests with her behind their back, it shows you're trying to do the same thing for her.

➢ **Don't ditch your old friends in the process.**

Perhaps you're so trapped in this wonderful new relationship that you slowly start bailing out your other friends. You feel relaxed with old friends, and it makes some sense, but it doesn't make perfect behaviour.

If you would like, invite other friends to hang up with you, but note that your other friends are important, so don't cut them out of your life, or let your new friend take high priority.

➢ **Don't hurry things.**

Researchers find that developing profound, loving partnerships is a marathon that is not a sprint and it's necessary to have a friend known as a romantic, slow and steady partner. So take your time! So take your time!

And remember: it should be enjoyable and somewhat thrilling to reconnect with a mate. Don't think it over and have a good time.

CHAPTER FOUR

Signs of A True Friendship

In the days of hundreds of Facebook 'friends' there appear to be few and far between true friendships founded on respect, mutual ties and memories in modern society. We can connect to anyone online automatically, but does this make them a tried and true friend?

On the other hand, your mates in real life could be as remote, flaky and untrustworthy as those in the cyber world you have linked to. Studies show that even if people have thousands of Facebook friends, in real life they only have close ties with a few.

1. They accept everything about you, including your flaws.

They don't want to change that. They don't want to change you. Really, true friendships mean they include all of you, including your peculiarities and flaws and your best qualities.

This does not mean that they like everything you do and do particularly or agree with it, but they don't even hate you or try to change your personality. You feel like a major stream of relaxation will flow through you.

That's because you met someone in a world of billions that treats you differently, even if you don't see them yourself.

2. They stick with you through both the good and bad times.

Perhaps this is easier for a false friend to separate from a genuine one; through difficult times a true friend wouldn't imagine that you're left alone in the dark. Instead, they promise to support you as soon as possible, and restore you to the light.

Fake friends always bail you out because they wanted to stick only when things were good for you, and think that it's a responsibility to them to help you with your issues.

3. They are happy for your successes and congratulate you when you reach a new goal.

Fake friends feel jealous and disdainful about your life, but true friends will enjoy their successes with you. Only note who's standing around as you hit a new height in your life to learn whether you have a true relationship or not. Some people will try to tear you down, but true friends are happy for you in your life.

4. You feel totally comfortable around them, and they probably know things about you that many others don't.

You find that you are all-round confident, know your best secrets and your wildest dreams and the extraordinary tricks you share only with someone you are the most secure with. You know yourself that many other people don't have them. Moreover, they are all aware of all the information of your sex life, your fond memories of your youth and all the awkward stories you should not share with anyone.

You want to meet you, not only on the top. This in many different ways divides a true friend from a fake.

5. True friendships meet you halfway – they don't expect you to always be the one to reach out to them.

You do not need to call or write each time you meet. This is also because you are interested in getting somewhere with you, and you will often be called to catch up. You do not feel like chasing them to keep them in your life–they make the same effort and time in your relationship. It's not just because you talk to them; it's that they genuinely care for you as a friend and want you in their lives.

6. They make you feel happier and more alive, not drained and stressed.

You make them feel more rejuvenated, optimistic and enthusiastic about life. You don't feel the opposite, but you've been watching them.

Authentic partnerships are a good energy fit for two people. If not, one person gives the other one power, that means you have an energy dragon in your possession. Just be careful how you act after meeting someone if you have a true friendship with them. A true friend, not discouraged and uninspired, can make you feel good about yourself.

7. They tell you the truth about things, even if you may not want to hear it.

True friends tell you what your hearts are, they never sugarcoat anything that will help you. Even if it could hurt, they tell you the truth.

And you have come to accept that because not many others will harass you perhaps say that it's the same in your career. They tell you that they don't cut you down, rather instead they help you take the best decisions in your life and thereby become a happier person.

8. They don't blow things out of proportion when you make a mistake – they forgive you.

You are not blooming out of the way when you are committing an error –you are forging yourself. Do not expect perfection from true friendships, because you are not going to expect that from you. You are going to expect consistency from true friendships. Furthermore, you don't believe you have to walk around them on eggshells trying to get their approval. You know that from time to time you can slip up and don't have to apologise for much. You just put it behind you and you know that despite whatever mistakes you might make, you have good intentions.

9. Real friendships mean they don't talk about you behind your back.

Real friends never whisper about you while you leave this place. In reality, if they have to speak to you, they behave as an adult and approach you directly. We respect you enough to avoid spreading lies and tarnishing your reputation;

we would rather smooth things with you and have fair face-to-face conversations.

10. They allow you to have other friendships without getting jealous and possessive.

You are all about to have other friends who do not have to use envy to try to control your life, and real friends feel comfortable in your relationship. You are free to pursue other hobbies and interests in your life because you know that your relationship is solid rock. You know you don't need to be in your business 24/7 to prove your relationship. We know.

11. You have so many inside jokes and funny memories with them that you've lost count.

You have had so many, you have so close friendship with them that you spend countless hours together, you have just stupidly and chuckled at nothing.

Friendships take your patience and love as well as any relationship.

However, the real sign that you have a friend for your life is that you really enjoy the time shared and expect your next touch.

Obvious Signs You're Hanging With the Wrong Friends

It's pretty much because being in the right crowd will make or break your career, because you know how good, how inspiring you are and how many milestones you achieve.

That's why a lot of people support the notion of being with the right friends and in a positive environment. However, it can be challenging. We don't want to let go sometimes. For both ourselves and others, we continue to make excuses.

We're blind to other times because we're in bad business. Take advantage and simply drop your toxic friends. They are anchors.

They are anchors. Rather than you can quickly meet new friends, you'll be better off without them.

1. They're making money a problem.

You steal, but if you do, never come back in time. Whenever the bill arrives, they miraculously vanish. You've got a job, so manage to get you paying for anything anyway. When you believe in your partnerships money contributes greatly to the skepticism, it is quite clear, frankly, that they are not good friends. You are seen as a wallet only.

Everything else, everything less. Nothing more. Remain with a community that is financially and otherwise supportive of each other.

2. They never follow what they say that they would do for you.

They're full of shit, in other words. Talk is so cheap that they are able to expend hollow words endlessly to keep you glad. It behaves and adheres to your word, which gives true character. You will never be betrayed for nothing by a real friend.

You don't need a mate who always takes you for granted. You're more than just words worth it. It's cheap talk that pulls you down (as it normally sounds so relaxed and reassured) So don't believe you even have to justify yourself with such a chat.

3. They're always too busy for you.

Simply put, nonsense is busy. Today, everyone's distracted. You're going to find the time because you want to spend time with something or someone.

No matter what. No matter what. If you have a friend always too busy to do, it is perhaps time to reassess the friendship, particularly if you have tried to spend time. Best to be in the company of people who are willing to be there for your sake. This is genuine friendship. True friendship. These are the real people who are always there for you.

4. They don't care about your struggles, only what your success can give them.

Why did friends say stuff like, "Wow do you make so much money? So Haha, I hope you have beers! "It may seem innocuous, but think of it. How critical are these friends about your successful journey? So much do they feel for you despite the wars and struggles you have experienced? If they simply don't care, when you need help, they will never be there for you.

A true friend wasn't just here, they'd be proud to see how far you have come.

In addition to this, friendship is about caring for each other, not how big their house is, or how much money they really are on the surface in terms of their standing.

5. They constantly pry on you so they can compare.

"How decent is your wages? "Have you been in bed for how long?" Oh, I bet that in my SATs I scored higher scores. What did you score? What did you score?"

The wrong guys have no grip on posing them, as disrespectful as these questions are. We don't know whether or not we make you uncomfortable. And what do you guess? You just don't know for the answers. In the expectation of being better than you, you just want to compare. And they'll just ask more annoying questions if they worry that they're not better. A good buddy should not feel awkward with each other. Nor do they compare. For each other, they are only grateful. You shouldn't have anything more to put up with.

6. They love the excitement and feed it.

That's when they're both chuckling and chattering. Virtual fights are available to the Whatsapp squad. We are bitchy and always pessimistic in their Facebook status. That drama will have effect in your life and would shock you. It's weary, exhausted and dishonest.

You wonder if they would one day turn the drama on you, or if they're thinking behind your back. Real friends are adult.

All of them are going to grow together and live like adults. Your life needs no extra drama, so stay away.

7. Because of them, you doubt the change in your life.

You are misunderstood friends should you ever have to doubt yourself, your attitude and your future with your friends. You can be strengthened by real and wonderful friendships.

They will make you so happy and encouraged you to wonder and even doubt how without them your life would work. Don't fool yourself. Don't kid yourself. Don't lie to yourself. Don't lie to yourselves. What you look, you know. There's nothing the questions can fix. Remove sails. Lower the anchors. Dump the mates into toxicity. Moving on to making new friends. That's going to be better in your life. More popularity would be gained, too.

Real Friends vs Fake Friends: Ways to Instantly Tell Them Apart

You say good friends are difficult to find. One person appears to be like a friend, but he is false. How can you tell the difference, between true friends vs fake friends? How do you say that: real friends versus imitation ones? Actually, it's not that complicated, all you have to do is take care of your acts. Lastly, however, you want to capture someone's true intention early. You can take that person out of your life in that way. You do not need them! You do not need them! In the first place, they're not your true friend.

So that's already a hint, if you're curious about the true intentions of a few people around you.

But if you want a more detailed explanation, this is how to differentiate between true and false things.

Usually, we grow up with a lot of peers around us. You've got people to hang out and laugh with, but it varies as we get older.

Your mates seem to be gone and to have a life of their own. Now, you cannot be friends with anyone, this is a part of life. But sometimes we pick mates with the best of their motives are not very close to us.

They might either have a nice time with you or help them pick chicks or guys. The point is, you really don't know. There will always be a bogus person who tries to sign for the ride.

1. You feel it in you.

For a cause, your intestine tells you something, and it's saying that you can't trust this individual. There's some explanation why the guard is up when you speak to someone you want to be a mate. Don't forget it, it's right. They're wrong if you think someone is false.

2. Once you hit the bottom, real friends are there.

Your life won't always be at a high level. Sure you will have a few fantastic moments, but there will still be a few lows. There can be any of your mates to rejoice, but if you hit the bottom of the rock and they're not there, this isn't a true friend. Your mates, with you, will be trapped in the bad times.

3. Fake friends treat you differently around certain people.

They can be sweet to you, but they are completely different when you're alone. It's a fake friend's sign. If they are around or not because they should not matter, they shouldn't treat you differently. If you need something, fake friends are good to you.

4. Behind your back, They 're talking.

Sure right, we sure prefer to do this. We're going to tell someone else if we're angry at our mate.

This is normal. This is usual. However, if somebody speaks poorly about you in order to disseminate lies and make people change their views, it is not a relative.

You won't talk terribly because you think about somebody.

5. Fake friends will be jealous of your accomplishments.

Naturally, without their benefit. However, once you found a new job with a higher pay, they would make snarky assumptions on it. They would definitely rejoice if you pay because, in truth, they aren't pleased with the results you've made. When you try to understand the distinctions between real friends and fake friends, note always that true friends are genuinely happy for you.

6. A good buddy is going to keep secrets.

If you tell a password to somebody, the intention is not to share it with others. A false friend takes this secret and uses it for his own personal benefit, whilst a true friend shuts his mouth and enjoys the fact that you share something intimate with him.

7. Real friends embrace who you are

A true friend doesn't care what you wear, or if you wear make-up. For whom you are, you love you. You don't have to act or dress to please them because this isn't friendship.

8. Fake friends only call you. When they need you

It is two different things to call someone to see what they're like and then call someone when you need something. Fake friends on Facebook or Instagram can be friendly with you, but only if they like you.

9. Real friends forgive you, No matter what.

It's unfair for everyone. And yes, you may have made a great error, but you will be forgiven by real friends. You don't want to torment you or use your disabilities as a tool against you. A real friend acknowledges the reasons and wants to be with you.

10. Fake friends don't like the word "no."

Well, really, who likes to hear "no?" That is not the point, however. If you don't give them what they want, a fake's mate will take the extra step not to stay with you. A true friend may not like to hear' no,' but they will keep up with you.

11. Real friends make time for you.

You can have two thousand friends on Facebook, so how many people would you call to watch a video or take a coffee? Two or three of them, maybe. True friends give each other time. Yeah, we are all busy lives, but you can always make a cup of coffee time.

12. True friends value your views.

We all have our own beliefs both politically and religiously. That does not say, however, it you can't be friends of someone else's thought. It contributes to the friendship, if anything. And if they disagree with you, a real friend values your opinions. There are various opinions and ideas in the world.

13. Fake friends don't care what you have to say.

Because they don't value your feelings, they don't matter. This is that they don't respect when they hang out with you but never listen to what you have to say. We all have mates that don't seem to be listening, either on their telephones or tuning out. Because they're not interested

CHAPTER FIVE

Things That True Friends Do

It can be difficult to distinguish between real friends and fake friends. They're very distinct, however! Real friends are the kind of people you can go to if you need something. In thick and thin, real friends are on your side. While your fake friends are the Earth's scum, they are going to offer you every service. It is important to know which kind of people you are playing with, the real ones, and those who are going to stand by you, regardless of what or not. It's critical to understand. These are some ways to distinguish between real and false mates.

1. Supporting your dreams.

True friends will motivate you to reach them and support you in your efforts. Your real friend will help you whether it switches your life entirely or taking on dance classes.

Your fake friends on the other side will only prevent you from being willing.

2. The forgive you when you make mistakes.

If the relationship is true, your partner would probably forgive or forget your errors and misunderstandings. There will be no negative or defiant thoughts. That's why they admire fellowship more than anything else.

3. Approving you the way you're

Real friends may be angry with you for a lot. But they won't judge you again. Real friends are going to be mad at you. You must embrace your path, and you appreciate your look pretty well. That's precisely why you guys were right friends? If you have a friend who wants to make a difference, realize that they're fake friends.

4. Standing up for you.

Real friends don't know how many relationships will become dishonest, but they will stand up for whatever. You want to be there to protect you from someone who wants to hurt you. Nevertheless, the phony are the imitators who will simply ignore and challenge you to deal with your own problems.

5. Your secrets are safe with them.

If you share secrets with them, it's nothing to think about. Share your deepest secrets and kindly understand you and keep them safe. Your anonymity is valued by real friends and you don't know if your secrets do not go out, even if you fight.

6. They keep in touch with you.

Bogus buddies will only be in touch with you if they want to hear a juicy gossip or need something.

Real amis are always involved in what is happening in your life, anywhere and every time.

7. They make time for you

It does not matter when they have an hour between work hours; a real friend will let you drink at all times! It's not money; it's a case of spending time with you and not time with yourself.

8. They make promises they can't keep.

You know a false friend when they are organizing for you. At the beginning, you're so glad. You're not going to hear from them then over time. Too sorry you are left alone for the entire moment. We won't even seem to fulfill everything. People like this tend to hear excuses, but they will not feel any guilt.

9. Gossiping about others.

If you have friends who chat nearly exclusively to others, the problem is how many they say behind the back. A true friend never would do that, true friends always have your back.

10. They only remember you when they need you.

You just want to know when you are born. You will still benefit from a false friend. They see you work hard, so they'll hop on and take advantage of the bandwagon. But a true friend is willing to return 100 times your generosity. Yet friends who don't just see you as a move. And once they do what they want, they'll tell you. Most of us often get caught up in a fictional fun honeymoon. But other things will inevitably be revealed, as if a relationship were real or fake.

Signs of Fake People to Look Out For

Seek to say the difference between a real night and a false human can be just as frustrating as attempting to find a distinction between an art piece and a well-made replica. Have you ever think a friend or even dating person has a secret agenda or just can't talk about your feelings and opinions.

➤ **They Only Respect Those in Positions of Power.**

Most would believe that everyone deserves this feeling when it comes to love. However, according to researchers, false people prefer to only value those in power.

➤ **They Work Hard to Build Relationships.**

While genuine people do not have to make extreme attempts to expand their friends ' circle, fake people can make an effort to earn other people's love. Friendship and other partnerships naturally come to interested people, but researchers suggest that synthetic individuals are less genuine in their formation of relationships.

➤ **They Seek Out Attention.**

Although it is all right to look for the spotlight from time to time, one indication of fake people is that they always look for publicity.

A true person probably knows, by comparison, when to make other people shine.

➤ **They Gossip.**

While a short talk session can encourage you sometimes, this is an experience that can help you find people who are fraudulent. Honest people are more ready to share their views publicly, while fake people will restrict their remarks to whispered.

➤ **They're Quick to Show Off.**

One point is that you are proud of your hard earned accomplishments, but it is a clear sign that you are a fake person. According to researchers, sincere people are modest and unselfish in perpetual pride.

➤ **They Put Others Down in Order to Look Good.**

Even individuals of clear credentials have to blame others for preserving their looks. In the name of making themselves look better, sincere people would rather respect and compliment others, while fakes will quickly put others down.

➤ **They Make Promises They Can't Keep.**

While a genuine person will do everything possible to satisfy his obligations and responsibilities, a fake will talk without going. Researchers say that false people are quickly committed, but rarely.

➤ **They're Only Nice If There's Something in It for Them.**

One who displays goodness only when it is helpful to a phony is a sure fire warning. Research points out, by contrast, that real people are genuine. No matter the circumstances, they are sweet and helpful. Keep a look at these signs of false people and encourage your lives to have real and positive relationships.

Signs Your Friendship With Someone Is Toxic

For intimate partnerships, abusive marriages should not apply. Friendships with others may sometimes be as manipulative and negative. A dysfunctional relationship can bring stress and resentment instead of taking your company and warmth to life.

1. There's a whole lot of drama.

One thing a toxic person can guarantee is drama. Chaos seems to somehow consume them, either because they disagree with someone and cause problems or because they keep happening unbelievable things.

"Drama is a big thing when we talk about toxic friends," A toxic friend appears to be somebody who draws us in either because it's very cool, very grandiose or because he's this miserable guy, who needs our support. "If your story you can bet that you will learn, or worse, get dragged into it.

2. Everything is about them.

A perfect way to test this is by discussing arbitrary subjects, which have nothing to do with either of you. A toxic person will have the uncanned ability to exploit the conversation back to them without skipping a beat, regardless of the subject.

3. They constantly put you down.

Toxic friend will never compliment you. They'll never pick you up or congratulate you on your achievements. In fact, they're much more likely to kick you when you're down. You'll realize you're never actually happy or relaxed around them because they don't make you feel good about yourself, No friendship should be transactional, but if someone is draining all your energy, you should ask yourself whether you're getting anything out of it at all.

4. They compete with you.

Whether it's your job promotion, a romantic partner, or a new class you're doing, your toxic friend will compete with you. They won't like the idea of you having anything that doesn't involve them, and they especially don't want you to excel at something. "They want to compete with you, even if you're not competing with them, "Even if you're in a completely different field, they want the same things you do."

5. They secretly copy you.

The competition can go one step further, and a toxic person will start to mimic you. They might buy the same bag you bought the week before, or start using the same slang words as you. "A very common thing I've heard, is this person really likes you, wants to spend all their time with you, and copies you," Researchers said. "So it's not uncommon for toxic friends to be very jealous of you, tear you down, and to some extent try to steal your identity. In severe cases, they might pretend to be you and use your photos, like catfishing."

6. They cross your boundaries.

Toxic people do incredibly inappropriate things. For example, Researchers said they may ring you on your house phone when you never gave them the number, or even show up uninvited. They won't listen if you tell them something they're doing makes you uncomfortable. Instead, they'll make you feel mean or crazy for even bringing it up. They have no respect for your space, and make you feel like you're abandoning them if you push back.

7. Toxic friends are obsessively needy.

According to research, you might feel like you've gotten yourself an obsessive boyfriend or girlfriend without even asking for it. They'll call and text you at all times of the day, even if you said you're busy.

"They want all your time, so it's a very codependent kind of friendship," she said. "So they'll text you all the time and expect a reply. Even if you say I'm going to be really busy over the next six hours, they'll text you just before, and throughout. And if you don't reply, they will kick up a storm."

8. They're jealous of other friends.

A toxic person will probably start to blame your other friends when you don't respond to their texts and calls. Researchers said they're likely to criticize your friends to your face, and try and isolate you from them.

"They are extremely jealous of your friends and will even go so far as to tell you you're their only friend, and you're the only person they care about, "Even if you're on a date they expect you to drop everything for them."

9. You feel responsible for them.

Even though they're acting unreasonably, toxic people are skilled at making people feel bad for them. Their guilt trips know no bounds, because they've probably spun a load of sob stories about how hard their life has been.

"You have this sense of support like you're a lighthouse for them, and if you collapse, they'll collapse," she said. "If you decide to spend your time with somebody else, what if they do something bad? If you don't answer them, what if they hurt themselves?'

10. They're hypocritical.

While they make you feel bad for not making enough time for them, toxic people won't ever feel bad for letting you down. But because they're so irrational and dramatic, you'll let them get away with it as you don't want to set them off.

"They might owe you money and pretend they never owed you, and rewrite history, "So you may feel irritated and angry, but because you don't want to trigger them and their difficulties, so you take a step back."

11. They lie to get sympathy.

Toxic people tend to inflate their backstory. "They may play up the chaotic nature of their lives to get sympathy," Researchers said. "They might tell loads of stories that make no sense, that don't quite add up." Still, always make sure to support a friend who constantly talks about drug use, alcohol problems, or abuse. Even the most toxic person might be secretly hiding a call for help.

12. You're always set up for failure.

Putting on public displays of drama are a toxic person's favorite activity. If you haven't done anything obvious toward them in a while, they might set you up for failure. For example, they could say you promised to go to the cinema with them and you stood them up, when that conversation never happened.

"They're very dramatic so they might publicly shame you in a place by screaming and shouting at you, so you feel bad and put in your place, "They make you feel like it's your fault if you don't want such behaviors, then don't do it again."

13. You'll feel something is wrong.

Researchers said your body is good at picking up signals that something isn't quite right. It can be hard to pinpoint exactly what it is that's wrong, but if you are constantly feeling on edge, it could be because there's a toxic person around.

"You cannot figure out what the hell is going on, "Your brain runs over time, and your mental energy is being sucked out by this person all the time. You don't only feel responsible, you feel destabilized around them. Some people make the room feel a bit energetically funny. Your body is a barometer telling you that they're trouble."

CONCLUSION

Friendship is one of life's most precious things. A friend means in your life, particularly in tough situations, you do not have to deal with it all alone. When you're sad, you'll be there to cheer, share your holiday days with you and be pretty much like a brother to you.

Sadly, not every friend of ours is accurate. They can only be friends with you because of your desire and you really know nothing, or just to kill you by chatting behind your back. They couldn't be friends with you.

We all share our happy and even craziest days with those special people in your lives. Such people make us forget that life is not necessarily a fairy tale but an exciting adventure; they are our soul sisters, friends, buddies, beasts, whatever funny and charming name that you call your unit. It's not a fairy tale.

While we hope to meet the right people, we often fall into the trap of encountering other individuals who do indeed meet the basic concept of a' friend,' but who do not always measure true friendship.

Fake friends are friends who don't know for our best interests. You will be spoken by this kind of buddy behind you. You know they are a sort of exploitation towards others, but you never knew they did the same to you.

These mates are poisonous. This is the kind of world we live in, we'll have mates like that. It's quite hard to tell if someone is a fake friend because most of them want to falsify their being fake friends as much as they can. You really are the fake.

False friends start out as someone who is interested in knowing you and is interested in your general wellbeing. This will be before the opportunity happens to you. Don't be surprised when this happens when you use your insecurities or other sensitive information. Emotional manipulators can use them against you easily and are well aware of your emotions.

Be mindful that when you begin to doubt a friend's sincerity, something is wrong. Confide in your thoughts.

HUMAN
ILLUSTRATIONS

In mind, we trust.

Printed in Great Britain
by Amazon

63624937R00035